METERED MOMENTS

Diary of a Cab Driver

Nipun Sharma

One Printers Way
Altona, MB R0G 0B0
Canada

www.friesenpress.com

Copyright © 2024 by Nipun Sharma
First Edition — 2024

All rights reserved.

I am honoured that I got to be part of these stories and my passengers share there stories with me. I dedicate this book to my passengers.

No part of this publication may be reproduced in any form, or by any means, electronic or mechanical, including photocopying, recording, or any information browsing, storage, or retrieval system, without permission in writing from FriesenPress.

ISBN
978-1-03-830628-9 (Hardcover)
978-1-03-830627-2 (Paperback)
978-1-03-830629-6 (eBook)

1. BIOGRAPHY & AUTOBIOGRAPHY, PERSONAL MEMOIRS

Distributed to the trade by The Ingram Book Company

Stories you all knew we had but you never got chance to hear from us-so here it is. This journey will take on different moods and experience but it worth it in the end. Stories of Vancouver.

TABLE OF CONTENTS

1	Introduction
3	A Bold Choice
7	A Full-Course Meal
11	A lady I met for a brief moment and she was inspiring
15	A Little Effort
19	A Musical Drive
21	A Passenger with a Big Heart
25	Egyptian Brother
29	A Young Traveler
31	Artist
35	The one where she sings.
37	Cliché
41	Constant Reminder
45	Don't Judge a Book by Its Cover
49	Connecting Dots
53	Learn to Let Go
57	Sincerity
61	What is Life without Friends?
65	Seoul-ful People
67	Sky High
69	Spiritual Seeker of North Vancouver
71	True Love
73	Perfect Ending

Introduction

I am pouring my heart into this book, sharing the experiences and countless lessons I have gathered over my years as a cab driver who relocated to Canada from India. Over the years, I have developed a habit of not talking to my cabbie friends and instead talking to the passenger. It's a simple idea—I don't like to feel left out, so why should I make my passenger feel that way? Let us embark on a journey together as I unearth some of these conversations from the land of memories.

We will encounter many different stories as you join me on the streets of the Vancouver area. I promise, you will be as joyful reading them as I was writing them. We are going to laugh together in this journey.

I am very thankful to you for reading my book, for witnessing my experiences. The passengers in the tales ahead became a part of me and took a little piece of me along with them. I hope the people in these narratives find my book and see my appreciation for them. I have always felt so grateful for meeting all of you. You all gave me the strength to make it to this point. There is no better way to show you thanks than by making you part of this book. I am honored for the opportunity my passengers have given me.

Thanks,

Nipun Sharma

1

A Bold Choice

This event left me in silence, processing what I'd just heard. A seemingly ordinary passenger but her strength and unwavering decision left a lasting impression, teaching me a powerful lesson about perspective.

I picked up a woman from her hotel. She was going to YVR—Vancouver International Airport. As usual, I started our conversation with "How are you doing, ma'am?" and "Where are you going?" She explained she was just heading back to the States after being in Canada for work.

She went on to tell me that she traveled a lot for work—more than two-thirds of the year, she was away from home, traveling.

"So," I responded, "it must be hard for your family, especially your kids, not seeing you that often."

She quickly corrected me. "No, I have no kids, and no husband, either—just two cats. I have someone taking care of them while I am gone."

We see the world through three lenses: our knowledge, our experiences, and our preconceived notions. After she said that she didn't have kids or a partner, I was quick to assume that she must be a divorcee, as though a woman her age must be married. Not just married—I thought she had to have kids.

Why did I assume that? Why was that the immediate thought in my head? Was I saying a woman was incomplete without a family and husband? It really struck me when I realized this assumption was wrong.

Back to her story. She told me she dated someone for long time, from her twenties to her thirties, and then they grew apart. She was not ready to get back in a relationship, so her frustration became her fuel, and she became fully invested in her career. After a few years, and with hard work, she achieved a good position in her profession and a comfortable lifestyle.

She said she did feel lonely sometimes, but now, with all she'd achieved, it was hard to lower her standards. After all, she'd worked so hard to get where she was. She would have to deceive herself to adjust to someone else's expectations, and she refused to do that. She chose to live her life on her own terms and stuck with that decision.

A woman is complete by herself, just as any other individual is complete in a marriage they are happy in. She was clear with what she wanted, and she seemed OK with her choices. I hope this book finds you ma'am, because I still remember you even after these many years.

We all have to make sure we are happy where we are. If you're not, then do what you need to do to make the situation happier for you. If you want to learn a new language, then learn. If you want to visit Luxemburg, then go visit it. Respect yourself just as you respect the people around you.

Come on—you owe it to yourself to make sure you are content in what you do. I know it's a big task, and it takes time and effort to get there, but keep at it. As I write this, I am

Metered Moments

doing what I enjoy, and I do it for hours. I have finally found my calling. **Find your voice. It's calling for you**.

A Full-Course Meal

Driving a taxi is one profession where you can never have the same day twice, but your objective remains the same. You might face hilly roads, or it might be raining cats and dogs, but you have to reach your passenger's destination and return home safely regardless of the situation. Sometimes, that means things get a little messy, and you just have to keep moving forward.

On Friday nights, I work. Sometimes, over the course of my twelve-hour shift, I only have time for one cup of coffee. At this time, rent was $200 (weekend nights were money-making nights, so higher rent), and gas usually ends up being around $25, so only after I have made $225 do I get any money. I work hard, moving in and out of downtown almost like a machine: you tell me the place, and I will get you there, no matter what.

On this particular Friday, I was getting close to about my sixth hour of work. I was around Hornby Street, and I saw a cab driver ahead of me leave behind two girls. I wanted to be their savior, so I pulled up and asked where they were going.

Do you know that feeling when you get a current crawling up your spine toward your brain telling you that you fucked up? Yes, that's just what I felt when I saw the condition of these two girls. They were both drunk, but one of them was fairly tiny and had drunk more than she could handle. Her friend, who was hoping to take care of her, was a good seven-tenths of the way to totally plastered but acting brave.

The friend got in first. The tiny girl was so drunk she couldn't even grab the door, but her friend made sure she got in. I asked once again, "Where are you going?"

"North Van," the friend answered.

I'm thinking, *Ooooo-K, this is gonna be rough,* but I ask, "Is your friend all right? She seems like she's done."

"Oh, no," the friend said. "She is just fine."

I prayed a little and then started driving, hoping it wasn't going to happen to me, the thing every cabbie dreads on a Friday night. We reached the West Georgia Street and Burrard Street intersection, and then I headed toward Lions Gate Bridge (LGB), keeping an eye on the backseat to make sure everything was OK, as I had a bad feeling.

I was speeding a little while driving through Stanley Park, trying to get rid of these passengers as soon as possible. As we gradually got to LGB, the tiny girl hit her limit and showed everyone everything she had drunk, as well as what she had had for dinner that night. The saddest part was, even though I couldn't see her throw up while driving over the bridge, she made sure I got my share, leaving a course of her half-chewed food and drinks on the seat of the cab and floor.

I was annoyed, but I didn't want to stop on the bridge, so I kept driving, hoping to get off LGB ASAP. I took an exit, pulled over, and told the tiny girl to get out and finish throwing up. She got out, but her friend said again, "Oh, no, she is just fine." I wanted to smack the "just fine" back into her mouth.

Metered Moments

They got back in, and I started driving, silently saying, "Shit." I told them my night was ruined—how was I supposed to work after that? And it wasn't even half a shift yet!

The tiny girl, Miss "Apparently Just Fine," said, "We'll pay you whatever we're supposed to. We're sorry." Her friend was probably in Lala Land.

Finally, we reached their destination. As I turned right to drop them off, Miss "Just Fine" threw up on the seat and on her friend. At that point, that seat had a full-course meal on it. I was pissed, but charged them the fare and the cleaning fee; they got out, and I left.

I went to a gas station, and the dude working there gave me a full roll of tissue paper and professional-grade cleaning spray. It took me thirty or forty minutes, but I cleaned up the backseat—or so I thought. I bought air freshener trees and hung them behind each seat, three in the back and one next to the front passenger seat, thanked the gas station clerk, my brother in late-night employment, and went back to work.

The next customers I grabbed were two guys. One sat where the tiny girl was sitting and the other one lay down on his lap and said, "My man, your car smells great."

"Thanks," I said, with a big smile.

I worked until 4 a.m. that day. I could still smell the sick, and I had a couple of keen passengers find leftovers in nooks like the door handle or the seatbelt lock, but I managed to work all night still.

In life, you have to do what you don't like. Life can't just be full of pleasant full-course meals. But you just have to deal with it—when you have to face a problem, just get it over with.

Nipun Sharma

When you want to make it work, you find a way to make it work. Keep at it.

P.S.—Sorry if you have lost your appetite.

A lady I met for a brief moment and she was inspiring

Brief encounters can be impactful—like this lady who cut me off as I tried to merge onto a road in the mountains. After making eye contact, we both sped up, continuing parallel for a few metres before she gave up and slowed down. As I looked back at her in the rear-view mirror, she taught me how ridiculous we look when we yell and gesture wildly at other drivers.

I picked up a passenger, who was in good mood. She was around Lafarge Lake and ran to my cab from the parking lot when I arrived.

As she entered, she told me she was in a rush.

"What seems to be the trouble?" I asked her. She said her friend was not feeling well and needed to go to the hospital. Though I can't recall what she said her friend's ailment was (my apologies), I could tell it was serious. I started driving right away toward her destination.

She told me that when she got the call about her friend, she was in the middle of a ten-kilometer run. I was shocked to hear that. I asked her if she had been running for a long time, and she told me she swam first, and was quite good at it.

Nipun Sharma

She used to swim twice a day, and then after getting married, she got busy with her family—she was the mother of four kids. Imagine the strength she has, being mother of four kids! Her oldest was going to university.

I told her running was special to me—it is in my blood, after all. My mother was an athlete until she got married to my father. My maternal uncle used to say that I and my older brother were nothing compared to her. Maa ran for her school and won so many certificates that she had a bag full of them. She used to tell me that she was selected randomly to run for her school, and once she started running, she started winning. It was like she found a hidden talent. She once ran in relay race with a high fever and she still came in second. She was known as a butterfly on her team for how fast she was on her feet.

I caught the running bug from Mom. I used to run and enjoy it to the point that it became meditation. I could run for an hour without a pause. Lately, however, I have been busy making money to make ends meet, so I can't find much time to run. With something like this, you might expect someone to say, "Eh, it is what it is." But just watch—I will go back to running.

I told the passenger all of this, and she was happy to know it. We had a good chat while the driving drama discussed at the beginning of the story happened; we managed to merge onto the road safely, and soon, we got to her stop.

"*Da svidaniya*," she said. "Keep running."

I was impressed by this passenger's strength—the kind of strength only mothers have. She had four kids, and though she didn't swim anymore, she could still manage a ten-kilometer run and also carry a heart to run to help in need. These

Metered Moments

dearest, sweetest, strongest, and most loving people have the strength to achieve so much and yet still just be our parents. (*I have stories for fathers, too—just wait*.)

A Little Effort

I usually avoid making conversation with people when they're not in the mood or don't seem comfortable enough to talk. After all, who am I to judge them? I usually pick up from body language if a passenger is in the mood for a little chat or if I should leave them alone. But it's easy to get lost in our own worlds, creating whole scenarios without even realizing that it's all happening in our imagination.

It was good day, as A) it was Friday, so everyone was generally in a better mood, and B) it was a busy day, and I had made good money so far. Next, however, I was in Tsawwassen, a suburban town where, in my experience, business can be hit or miss. Sometimes I go there and I get a passenger making a long trip off the ferry right away, and sometimes I end up walking in the mall for an hour before I get any passengers. I feel, though, that the expectations you set up inside play out exactly on the outside, at least for the most part.

Even in Tsawwassen, I was getting passengers consistently, and I was making money. I soon got sent a passenger because of her name, which kind of sounded like an Indian girl's name. That's just what I found when I picked her up—an Indian girl who just got off work. She got in, and I asked how her day was. She was getting off, of her first job and heading to her second

15

job. She started working at her first job at 8 a.m. I picked her up around 1:20 p.m., and she said she was scheduled to work the second job until 8 p.m. I asked her why she was working so hard, and she responded, "You know we have to."

We accept things in life without giving them much consideration sometimes. She found it so normal to work two jobs every day, yet some people just work one job and complain about how hard life is and how they're not paid enough.

Life is what you make of it. We are not living in a country in a warzone, and we are not under surveillance twenty-four-seven. I say this from my perspective without meaning to disrespect anyone. In Canada, the average person working nine to five can live a good life. We need to appreciate that. We have freedom of choice.

I asked her if her immigration process was complete yet.

"No, not yet," she responded, but she seemed optimistic about it.

There are two takeaways here. The first is that, after five years of living in Canada, she worked hard, working two jobs, but she wasn't stressed about it. There are people like her who started in the same place and at the same time as you, but now they are ahead. You don't need to stress about things that are not in your control.

Second, it is OK to solve this puzzle of life at your own pace. Ditch the comparisons, focus on your own journey - fuel your motivation, and build self-respect.

I have had multiple jobs over the years and now I think all those jobs were needed to make me the person I am and experiences helped me to make better decisions for the future.

Metered Moments

She asked me about my life, and I told her that I was not married yet, but my parents were being creative every day. Every time we spoke, they had a new relative asking me if I was getting married anytime soon. She said it was getting to that point for her, too. We both laughed. Even though we were almost a decade apart, we still had the same issues. Maybe these were human issues we all face, and we should take a chill.

We got to her work, a Tim Hortons location. Since I was still working without breakfast at 1:30 p.m., I decided to grab a bite there. As she stepped out of the car, I followed her. She looked at me for a second, and I told her I was just grabbing a brunch. Inside, she started her shift, and when no one took my order for a minute, my passenger decided to take my order. When I pulled out my phone to pay for it, she said not to worry—it was on the house. I told her I didn't mind paying, but she just said, "Don't worry, I got it." I got my brunch after few minutes, and I thanked her and walked away.

A simple conversation of five to ten minutes made her comfortable enough to buy me brunch. It was a small gesture on her part, but take a second to think about it. When was the last time you bought a stranger food or a cup of coffee; they could afford it, but you still get for them. We all are equipped with decency and etiquette. ***I firmly believe in treating people around you as you want them to treat you***.

A Musical Drive

This is one of my favorite rides! I'll probably remember it forever, at least as long as my brain functions correctly. This ride was like a magical, musical adventure of a cabbie—a cabventure!

I was working an all-nighter, from 5 p.m. to 5 a.m. It was a very comfortable shift. I had the great benefit of still managing to get six to seven hours of sleep while working twelve hours a day, as well as one hour for a walk, and then another walk after a lunch break at work.

It was 2 a.m. and I was in Kitsilano to pick up a passenger. I got to the pick-up spot, and this lady came out looking like she was coming from a wedding or like she had gotten married herself. She got inside my cab, and it turned out she was going to Coquitlam, "so it's a long one" (in her words).

I started talking to her, asking how her day was. She told me that she was at her friend's wedding and she was one of the bridesmaids, but now she was dead tired. Then, she said, "If you don't mind, I would like to play my ukulele."

"It would be my pleasure," I responded.

She took out her ukulele from the bag she'd brought in with her. "I'm tired, so I'm going to shut my eyes as I play, but can

Nipun Sharma

you please go straight where you need to go without driving me extra?"

"Relax and trust me," I told her. Driving her home was already a treat for me; why should I bother her for a couple more bucks? She wouldn't enjoy playing if she were stressed about my taking her on a longer route to make money, and if she didn't enjoy it, then I wouldn't either.

Live music has a particular charm to it, I had goosebumps as she played. I didn't record her or anything—I just enjoyed it.

The thing about late-night drives is that if you enjoy driving, you will find them almost meditative. I was simply enjoying this drive as she played live music in the back. The moment had a warm feeling, that happiness inside, like when in winter you wear freshly washed night clothes that still have a little warmth in them from the dryer. Or that joy for people who wake up early for work and have the first sip of their tea or coffee. That's the feeling I had, but for forty minutes.

Pure joy. That's what it was. Today, we are so eager to capture the moment for later that we forget the whole point to be in that moment and enjoy it. Live each moment so when you look back, you will see a fulfilling life with no regrets and a sense of achievement. In addition to the beautiful music, that's what the ukulele bridesmaid gave me—***that important reminder***.

A Passenger with a Big Heart

This time we are going back further in the past. I have been driving for a long time, so you can be sure my trunk is full of memories. This story is very special—I hold it dear to me, replaying it for myself just as we go back to special shows and movies from time to time.

I picked this guy up from the cruise terminal on a bright, hot summer morning, the kind where the sun seems to be right down here with us. This was a trip of three people. One older gentleman sat with me in the front, and the other two sat in the back. I started driving through busy Howe Street and was happy to take them to the airport. However, I had forgotten my sunglasses at home, and as it was 11:30 a.m., the sun was shining brightly. Since I was so used to wearing these glasses, it felt especially so.

The passenger in front started talking to me. "So, how's business? How's your summer going?"

I am always up for conversation, so I replied, "Yeah, it's good. Cruises are important for Vancouver, and we cab drivers get a lot of business there."

We kept chatting as we drove, and, thankfully, the trip to the airport was the best we could have hoped for, so we were all in a good mood. I was telling him the usual stuff—that Vancouver was almost heaven, though I wished it was a bit cheaper. He was a friendly old man, and was heading back to Calgary. Though he was old in looks, he was young at heart, and we laughed the whole ride away while the passengers in the back were busy with their own dialogue.

I took the exit toward the entrance for departures and stopped at the domestic terminal. The old passenger was happy with our little chat, and I was happy to have been of service.

"So what's the damage, son?" he asked me as he stepped out of the car. I told him it was thirty-three-and-something dollars, and he opened his wallet, gave me fifty dollars, and said, "Keep the change." I was so happy to receive that seventeen-dollar tip. I got out of the car and started unloading their luggage. While the other passengers grabbed a buggy for their suitcases, I got their luggage out and helped them set it up.

Before leaving, the old passenger stopped to say, "Thank you for the pleasant ride" and shook my hand. This was obviously the pre-COVID era when there were no masks fogging up specs and hand-shaking was a thing. While he shook my hand, he said, "It seems like it's going to be a beautiful sunny day," and took off his sunglasses and handed them to me. "You need these more than me."

I was shocked, and his kindness was beyond words. I resisted, but he insisted so I accepted.

I wore his glasses to make him happy. He was so glad, and so was I. He walked away and I went back to my car.

This feeling we shared, him and me felt, was like a kindness overload, pure joy. In my opinion, the people who believe in a higher power, or God, or God's messengers, or a creator,

Metered Moments

whatever you may hold sacred—that feeling of a mighty, omniscient force—must resemble this. Here's what I mean: God is in joy, in good feelings.

If you want to feel that, just try this. One day, start treating the world the way you want to be treated. If you can help someone out, then do it, but with no expectation of return. Just simply do it and watch that person be happy. When I am in those little moment of happiness, it feels like I am closer to God. I hope I am making some sense to you all.

That very same day, after working for the whole day with the good feeling of that trip, I met this other guy who needed a ride from Vancouver's Amtrak train station. He had come by train from Saskatchewan with his bicycle, and was having trouble getting a cab because his bike was too big. He came to me, and I said, "If it fits, then I can take you."

We both carefully tried, and I managed to make it to work. It was a short trip, maybe fifteen minutes. When he got out of the cab, I helped him with the bike, and as he was about to leave, I said, "You know, it's a sunny day. Would you like some sunglasses?" He said yes, and I gave him the old passenger's glasses. He smiled as he put them on, and then he rode his bike away.

I gave him those glasses because I wanted to feel the joy the older passenger must have felt when he gave them to me. I know they were a gift, but once again, the biker needed them more than me. As least I was still in the car—he was in the open on his bike, and plus, I had glasses at home. The most important thing, though, once again, was that joy, the joy of helping someone without any expectation. **Kindness is the key here. Kindness**.

Egyptian Brother

This was one of those days where I decided to work extra-long hours—something like thirteen hours. I was on the last leg of my shift, my hunger was growing, and I was getting tired. Just as I bought a coffee from Tims and was wondering if I should head home, I received a pickup request from the domestic arrival terminal. I accepted it without thinking twice.

After grabbing my coffee, I went to the domestic arrivals area. A mid-forties man with a child and lots of luggage came forward. His luggage made me nervous, as I wasn't sure if it would fit. I told him as much, but he wanted me to try. He didn't say so, but honestly, I can usually read my passenger's expressions, and his said it all. I tried fitting as much as I could, and in the end, we managed to stick all his luggage in the trunk and packed his two backpacks with him inside.

We started the drive. He was going to UBC, and en route, he started asking me questions and shared his story as well. He was moving with his family from Egypt. He told me where he was going to work and asked me if it was an easy commute from his residence. I suggested a few areas that would be better. As he was a new immigrant, he was dependent on public transport, so he had to live closer to work.

25

Nipun Sharma

His son was fluent in English, but still very young—maybe seven years old. I was very impressed with this young gentleman. His father and I laughed at his observations. Conversations are such a magical, yet simple, way to connect to anyone, regardless of their age, color, background, ethnicity, or political beliefs.

Amongst his son's comments, this passenger told me about Egypt and his life there. I explained how I loved the culture in Egypt, and how I was very fascinated with Cairo and would like to go there one day.

As he and I chatted, I gave him my best knowledge of Vancouver and told him a few things he needed to be careful about. Then I gave him the suggestion that I give to anyone who moves here from anywhere: I suggested to move to a cheaper place than Vancouver. As a new family starting to adjust, it would be hard to settle in a new city when it was so expensive. Making ends meet would be hard, especially if they wanted a house for their family.

It's about perspective; any immigrant in Canada comes here with the very simple idea that there's a better quality of life available. But if you buy a house as new immigrants, it will be years before you find yourself somewhat settled. Your work will just go straight to bills. Living somewhere cheaper will give you the opportunity to spend less time working and more family time. Parents should be able to watch their kids grow. It's what every parent deserves. It's about the journey.

He was very happy with my suggestions, to the point he said he was glad he found me as a driver (his words). The pleasure was all mine. If my suggestions and knowledge help you to make some positive changes, I am more than happy to

Metered Moments

talk to you—even if it means we are already at your destination but keep talking for an extra five minutes before we finish up the trip.

That man and his son left me reflecting. Parents do everything for us. This Egyptian father left everything behind so he could give his son a better life. We don't realize that that's the biggest sacrifice anyone can make for someone they love.

It's not just parents—it could be anyone who goes out of their way to help you. They deserve your respect. A friend, a cousin, a teacher, or a complete stranger. Let's all remember that what makes us human is the human experience. We have the ability to sense each other's needs. Next time you see a person in need, lend a hand, regardless of how big or small a help you can offer. It can have a long-lasting impact on someone's life. ***Lend a helping hand***.

A Young Traveler

This should be considered a prime example for people who underestimate our youth. Youngsters are usually seen as inexperienced and careless, but they often prove this judgement wrong.

It was one fine afternoon in Vancouver in the month of July, and it was cloudy and rainy, as expected. There came a young passenger, one an age at which you feel if you try hard enough, you will rule the world. This trip was a scheduled one, and he was a few minutes late.

I started driving, and, for some reason, I hate going downtown after 1 p.m. It seems like everyone gets off work at once, clogging up the roads. After driving a few blocks, I asked, "Hi, how are you doing? What do you study?"

He said he was good, and that he was going to drama school at UBC and had directed a grad film. "I want to be a director one day," he explained. "I know it will take time, but I will enjoy my journey."

We talked about a few other things, and then he said that he meditated every day in the morning for twenty minutes. Well, at that, I had to ask if he was reading anything, and he told me he was reading some spiritual books. I told him I was reading Kahlil Gibran's *The Prophet*. He seemed interested, and wanted to note the book's name. I also told him about *The Will to Power* by Friedrich Nietzsche and, my favorite, *Apprenticed to a Himalayan Master* by Sri M.

Next, I asked, "Have you ever been meditating, then felt like crying?"

"No, not yet," he said. "I am just trying different meditations, and when I am in deeper meditations, I feel very light." I told him to keep meditating (though I needed to start myself), and he said he would. I told him to have a good day and I left.

This kid was doing meditation at only twenty-three years old. His views on the world seemed more intelligent than many adults' today. He had a curious mind, and was interested in the arts of looking within.

We should all take a cue from this passenger and look within once a day. Our introspective battery pack goes down by the end of the day. You have a very finite amount of energy to give. Why are we wasting our energy on things and people we don't give a damn about? Just stay charged with a smile, be good with people, and be the best version of yourself. You know why? Because who else is going to take care of you?

Relax. It's not "You versus the World." What's usually going on inside is actually "You versus You." Let's be gentle with ourselves so we can be at peace within. **This will lead to peace everywhere.**

Artist

This story is something we all need to hear. We all do things that we don't enjoy, and we keep doing them because they make us feel safe and secure. Maybe it's a job you've been at for years, it feels like you know everything about every person at work —whether you like them or not, they are familiar. Despite the dislike, you still do what you gotta do!

This guy must have been very strong, or at least so frustrated with his situation that he decided to do what most of us don't have the courage to do.

It was the weekday afternoon rush, and I was working. I was picking up passengers during this time most early morning workers were clocking out . I picked a passenger up at one of the VFX studios we have in Vancouver. I love getting customers from this line of work because they have inside information on upcoming movies. I love movies, so if they can give me any details, I want to know! I remember I had one passenger who told me that he worked on Thanos's Infinity Gauntlet. I also met a guy who told me he worked on *Black Panther* and couple of other big projects.

On this day, I asked my passenger, "So, how is work for you these days?" He told me it was busy. I followed up, asking if he liked his job. He said, "Yes, man. I love it. It's a standard nine-to-five kind of job for me, so I get to go home in the evening, and weekends are off."

Someone who already works in these conditions wouldn't get that excited about such a basic thing. I guess because we take it for granted, so we don't find it as big of a deal to get evenings and weekends off. Then there are people like me who would ask if we could make the weekend three days long instead of two days. You might think people like me are a minority, but we are growing.

He started telling me that, before his current job, he was a sous chef for thirteen years. "I loved that job," he said, "creating meals for people that made them happy. It was a fun environment, but it came with its own challenges."

I have the utmost respect for chefs, as I worked as a trainee chef for a year in a five-star hotel. Being a chef is one of the most honest professions, in my opinion. You cannot lie—you can either cook or not cook. It's simple. I remember a quote I heard in a Bollywood movie: "Chefs are complete artists because the art we create attracts your eyes, attracts your nose when you smell it, attracts your ears while you hear preparations; then you taste the food, and it makes you smile." A complete art—I couldn't agree anymore.

While being a chef is great, there's also a lot of problems. The days you want to take off and spend time with your family are the days you are the needed the most at your work—weekends, Thanksgiving, Halloween, Easter, summer breaks, spring breaks, and, to top it all off, Christmas. A chef is supposed to work all these days as people like to eat out for these special occasions. Chefs also can usually barely survive on their pay, despite the ten-to-twelve-hour days they have

Metered Moments

to work on average. This is the reason a lot of chefs end up leaving this field.

This passenger was an inspiration. After being a chef for thirteen years, when he must have been so comfortable in his position and with his colleagues, he chose to fix his life. He went ahead and took a loan to study VFX. After obtaining his diploma, he got a job and successfully switched his career. Most of us can't even imagine starting all over again.

Chef to VFX artist—I think this guy teaches us a lot. You aren't in a race; it's never too late to change your life. He was now happy getting to go home at the end of the day and having weekends off. Having the courage to make a choice is difficult—we're often hard on ourselves and get unmotivated. This guy was able to bring about the change he wanted in life. ***But one thing remained the same: he was creating an art, whether he was a Chef or in VFX.***

The one where she sings.

Music plays a big part in our lives. It can be hard to choose a particular favorite song (honestly, I think it should be prohibited to ask someone to choose a single favorite). However, many of us have songs that are particularly special to us and connect to a special moment in our lives.

This story is very musical and inspiring. As dusk strolled in and the sun took off, I went to pick up a customer in Langley. When I arrived, she was carrying quite a bit of luggage. I assumed it would be an airport trip, but, nope—it was to Burnaby. Not bad! I settled her luggage in, got back in the cab, and drove off.

I asked her how her day was and why she was traveling between cities, noting her big bag. She was a happy spirit, and spoke with a lovely British accent. She giggled a little and said, "Sorry (for the big luggage), I was here for work and now I'm heading home." She worked a corporate job, but she was still smiling at the end of the day; hats off to her!

She started telling me she'd moved here from London, England, with her family, whom she lived with. As she was English, I told her that I loved Adele. She asked me which song was my favorite, and I said "Someone Like You." She said that was her favorite too.

She asked me about my job, saying that I must meet a lot of interesting people. I said yes, and that the people were great. Good people are out there—polite and respectful.

"I've had some great experiences in cabs," I told her. "One passenger sang for me, and she was from England as well"—another musical story I'll have to tell another time.

"I like to sing as well," she said as I entered Burnaby. "I sing because it makes me happy." I told her I sang too, but it was better if she didn't hear me sing for the safety of her ears.

After a brief pause, she said, "You know, I would like to sing for you as well."

"That would be my pleasure," I responded gladly. To my surprise she sang my favorite song, "Someone Like You." She sang beautifully. I almost could have asked her to sing once more, but we were almost on her street. I requested that she continue her career as a singer. "I want to see you on stage one day," I told her.

"You will," she responded.

We all are strangers to each other, but if we never gave these strangers a chance, we wouldn't have friends, and without that, we would miss out on love, companionship, experiences that we will remember for a lifetime. Conversations make a deep impact on our lives. **To begin these conversations, the first step is KINDNESS.**

Cliché

We all carry smartphones with us, and they provide us with an avalanche of information on a daily basis, whether we need that info or not. Most of the things we consume on our phones are repetitive, so they really don't give us the stimulation we are looking for. Some of the things we found exciting on our phones at first we don't even blink an eye at anymore.

A similar issue with repetition happens with clichés. They might be a piece of advice or a line spoken that we have heard many, many times. If we hear it again, we won't even give it a second thought, let alone let it intrigue us enough that we question ourselves and try to become better people.

The trip in this story was a short ride, but I realized its importance after the customer reached her destination. Why did it take me that long to realize how important it was? The same reason I mentioned above—it was a piece of information that I had heard so many times; it didn't interest me anymore. This time, however, it came from someone who wasn't just saying mere words. Rather, it was someone who lived and suffered through something and learned a hard truth that, to other people, might have just seemed like a clichéd line.

Nipun Sharma

It was a sunny Thursday in March. We still had some snow on the sidewalks, but the roads were mostly clear. Driving under the bright sky, I received this customer's trip request.

I was informed that her location was a little tricky—it had caused issues for me the last time I went there, as well. There are these townhouse complexes next to each other, and in the one she was in, the address board was hidden unless you completed the turn and tried to go inside. Uber's map is hit or miss—sometimes it takes me to the precise location of the passenger, even if they are standing in a parking lot, and sometimes it is off by twenty blocks. I took a chance and followed the Uber map, and, luckily, it was right this time.

I got to her place and she was waiting for me, wearing a mask and hat. She got in and I asked her how she was doing. She said she was doing well and was going to work, explaining that she was a nurse.

"That's a hard job," I told her. "I mean, twelve hours a day, you're surrounded by someone near their last breath, someone about to give birth, and people everywhere in between. In a nutshell, it's a lot to handle for me."

"Yeah, it can be challenging, she said, "but I enjoy it. I'm happy to go back to work."

I asked her if she was going back to work after a day off, to which she responded, "No, I was at home for months. I got tired of being at home, so I asked to go back to work. I had a tumor in my brain. They removed it, but the process is hard on the body, so I couldn't work."

"That must have been hard for you," I said. "Do you have any family around?" She explained that her nearest relative,

38

Metered Moments

her mother, lived in Miami, but that the rest of her family was in the Philippines.

"Well, then," I asked her, taking everything in, "how have you been doing?"

"I'm a bit better, but I miss my hair." She took her hat off, showing me her head. "I know it looks badass"—and it did, she had a mohawk—"but I miss my hair."

She went on, explaining that the tumor was not curable and might happen again. She also told me that going through the treatment was hard on the body.

"Sometimes I needed to get to Vancouver for my appointments, and I would be so tired and need rest after them, making travel hard. But I knew someone who died in eleven months after finding out they had a tumor in their brain. I'm alive, so I am happy."

She looked out the window. "If I stay at home, though, I'll go crazy because all you do it just worry about everything. That's the last thing I want to do."

I said I totally agreed. She went on, telling me she was not allowed to travel for long hours, which meant she couldn't leave the city. She wasn't allowed to fly, either, so she couldn't go to her family.

At this point, she said her procedure was almost complete. She wasn't technically allowed to work yet, but on her request, her work was letting her go in twice a week.

"Life is too short," she said. I had heard that line many times before, so the impact of it on me was minimal. But she continued, saying she now understood that phrase, as she had to recover from treatment and live with the constant fear of her tumor coming back.

We reached her work and I dropped her off, telling her that her mohawk looked great so she should keep it. She laughed and walked away.

As I drove from this passenger, a realization struck me harder than before that life is so unpredictable. Two days prior, on a Wednesday night, I had called my father. He told me he was on his way to a co-worker funeral. The worker, a young man of forty, had passed away. This current passenger, I noticed was thirty-nine who survived this tumor. A strange somber connection formed in my mind.

There is a story in my religion: when a king was heading toward heaven, he was asked, "What is biggest lie you came across in your lifetime?" He said, "People die every day, but still we believe that it's not going to happen to us, even though we very well know our clocks are also ticking. Yet we still shut our eyes and think we are going to be fine."

If we remind ourselves that we all have limited time on this earth, we will live a different life. We will take chances on ourselves. We will forgive quickly and apologize even quicker. We will take that trip and make all the necessary decisions that we have been putting off for whatever reason. ***Remember this story, and remind yourself every day that life is too short***.

Constant Reminder

We all love a beautiful story and you will be surprised where you can find a story that can change your perspective on life completely. I came across one, so here it is.

This story is like that. It is a story of a fierce woman who lived her life to the fullest. She was an excellent photographer and doctor. She had a big and beautiful family and a loving husband, and I learned about her in my cab.

It was a Wednesday, and I was working downtown around 1:10 p.m. It was a gloomy day. I got a trip request from a lady going to senior care. I picked her up, and I asked her, "How's life?" She said she had two kids and family life was going well. Our exchange continued as follows:

Me: Is this another work trip?

She: No, I am going see my mother. She lives in senior care.

Me: How is she doing?

She: She's doing OK, but she's old now, and it's catching up to her. She has dementia, so she forgets things often.

Me: I am sorry to hear that. I hope she gets better soon. Are you the only child?

She: No, I have a brother too. He and I come as much as we can. She doesn't remember how to take care of herself, if she has any money, or if she can afford where she was staying.

Me: Her memory is that bad? Does she remember her past?

She: She asks me sometimes, "Who took this photo?" And I tell her, "You, Mom." You know, she was an excellent photographer. She also worked as a doctor for the longest time. She is a strong woman.

Me: So you and your brother make time for her. Do you take along your family, too?

She: Yes. My girls are in school today. Otherwise, I would bring them along. My brother also tries to bring kids.

Me: How is she now? What does she do all day?

She: She's good. At the home, they have fully planned days for them, from breakfast to room clean-up to walks and group activities and naps. We also go every week. But you know, she gets the happiest when someone brings her French fries. She just love French fries from McDonald's.

Our conversation drew to a close as I dropped her off at her destination. I stopped for a second and just stared at the place, a care home where you live away from everyone you know and your house. You cannot make decisions for yourself, but you are living still. Is all the stress your little heart has taken on, gone now because there's no work? No more late-night shifts—it's just you.

Consider yourself lucky if you still have a partner by then. If they can still bear you, then you both deserve a gold medal.

I mean in the end, while we are chasing our dreams, those little moments of happiness we all get we have to make the best use of. Sit down sometime and take a deep breath. Grab

Metered Moments

that fancy dinner you think is overpriced. Enjoy it with that cheap wine you like. Tell your parents you love them because tomorrow, they might not be there to hear it. Tell your partner you love and appreciate them, give them a kiss on the forehead. Speak to that brother you haven't spoken to in a while. Who cares who said what last time? Grab your dog and take a walk or just cuddle in bed. Water your plants, help someone, just listen. It seems like everyone is speaking. No one wants to listen. Catch up with that friend who was once so close to you that it hurts now.

Before you become someone in life, become yourself.

Don't Judge a Book by Its Cover

I know this is another cliché, but it's another one that's important in life. We all seem to have built a world in ourselves. We see things our own way and have confidence that the way we see things is the correct way. It comes as a surprise when something you thought was a certain way, something you never bothered to inquire about, turns out to be another way entirely.

Someone asked the Dalai Lama once why there was so much dissatisfaction in this world, why people were not content even though they had more than people had fifty years ago.

The Lama said that we are self-centered, and we often create statements about everything in our minds, and we go on living life by those assumptions rather than double-checking them. Things are not as you think they are. We don't see things as they are, we see things as we are, and there is a big difference in there.

Philosophy break's over—let's get into the story, which is a perfect example of the title I've given it. Let's take you on the ride.

Nipun Sharma

It was a sunny summer day in 2017, and I was working downtown. I got a call from the west end to pick up a young Asian girl. The encounter turned out to be a memorable one.

I assumed she was from somewhere in Asia and probably moved here alone. She was heading to Richmond, and I started driving once she got in. I asked her how she was doing. She said good, she was heading for lunch with some friends; life was going well, and she was keeping busy.

When I asked her where she was from, she told me she was originally from Thailand. She said she had moved after Grade 12, and it had been a few years since she arrived.

Then she told me she had been to India and lived there for a few years. I was surprised—she was there for schooling, from Grade 6 to Grade 10, at a school in Darjeeling. An aside—you guys should check Darjeeling out. This place is like the go-to spot for all the Bollywood romantic movies.

She told me she studied at a boarding school there, and she learned Hindi, the language spoken by most people in India. She also used to watch Bollywood movies all the time, and Shah Rukh Khan was her favorite actor (mine too). I almost didn't believe her, but she did mention a few movies she'd watched during her stay in India. The icing on the cake was that she spoke a few words in Hindi too. She told me she still watched Hindi movies on Netflix and without subtitles. I was impressed and in shock.

We reached her destination, and she disembarked. I said good day, still in shock, but I was genuinely happy to have met her. If I hadn't spoken to her, she would have been just another passenger to me, someone going from point A to point B. I would have made peace after my assumptions about her as an Asian girl. But after just a simple conversation, she

Metered Moments

changed the whole scenario. So, in my opinion, and I hope yours too, she showed that things aren't always as they seem to you, and it's always worth actually opening the book to learn more about it.

(Ps: You guys should check Darjeeling out, Its beautiful)

Connecting Dots

This trip was one of the most interesting ones I have ever had. I started from 1st Avenue in Tsawwassen and went all the way to North Van. My passenger wanted to grab coffee, and in my six years of driving, this was the first time my passenger and I grabbed coffee while on a trip. He seemed like an interesting guy.

After grabbing our choice of poison, we embarked on the hour-long journey to North Van. He seemed like he had a hyper personality. He told me he was going to work, so I asked him why he lived so far away from his job. He told me that he lived with his friends. He enjoyed living with people his age; they all liked each other and got along well. He said they were all hard-working people that had goals in life and wanted to achieve big things. His friends were his source of motivation, but when they went out for work trips, they somehow took his will to work as well.

He said that he was, as I thought, a hyper individual. He liked going out to parties, and clubbing and escort services were always on the menu. He apparently owed a bunch of money to his friends due to this lifestyle, so he hoped to work hard and pay them back as soon as possible.

I told him that we all had our demons to fight and that he shouldn't be too hard on himself. He should appreciate that he had such people around him to support him, but at the same time, he should learn to take care of himself. After all, if you are not going to support yourself, who is going to do it for you?

As we passed through south Vancouver, he told me his mother lived there by herself. I asked him about his father, and he told me that his parents separated when he was really young. His father had bipolar disorder, which affected this passenger's childhood as well.

I told him we all struggled with things in our own way. Human beings don't talk anymore; you might feel alone while everything is happening to you, yet the person sitting next to you could very well be in the same situation as you. We need to first respect ourselves. We tend to do things for others out love or respect or friendship, yet we fail to show up in that same way for ourselves. We never miss a chance to be hard on ourselves, when we don't do what was needed. We create a cloud of despair that steals our sunshine, our hope, and our strength. The icing on the cake is that we then do even further damage to ourselves by ending up feeling guilty about how we messed up. We don't even realize how much we hurt ourselves this way.

We tried to turn the conversation to something more positive, and he told me that he did sales for his company and thought he was a good talker because he could do sales door to door. We all have talents that we can find and work on, and I told my passenger I was sure he was good at other things too.

Metered Moments

At that prompt, he told me that he enjoyed making music and that he was Japanese, from a small town on the south side of Japan. I told him I had a certain fondness for Japan—once it is mentioned, I have a whole list of things to talk about. I had been there twice, liked sushi, and LOVED anime. He recommended I marry a Japanese girl from Japan, saying they were sweet, caring, and trustworthy. "Sure, I said, "maybe in my next life."

Now that we were connecting a little more, he said, "You know what? I feel that every man's dream is to work hard, make money, and then sit somewhere in the mountains and meditate." This hit me hard—that's what I felt. I often thought about how I wanted to try meditating in the mountains one day.

I told him about my love for anime and lately how obsessed I was with it. The passenger said he didn't watch anime anymore. I told him that I started in 2021 but had seen all the big guns already. I felt I understood them all in a different way. We can learn a lot from anime, or any story, if we change our perspective a little. When we watch anime, even when the main character is struggling against impossible odds, we have an unquestionable belief that they are going to make it, and they eventually do. Why don't we have that same confidence in ourselves? We are the main characters of our lives, after all.

As we approached his destination, he said, "Man, I enjoyed talking to you. Can I get your Insta or something?"

I told him sure, he could take my number and get in touch if he thought of anything else he wanted to discuss.

He shook my hand. "If you don't mind, can I send you the music I make? You can give me an honest criticism." I said it would be my pleasure.

To the person from this story—I pray that you find what will interest you for the rest of your life. You have a lot of potential. All of you who are reading do as well.

Dattebayo.

Learn to Let Go

The passenger in this story reminded of something I had learned through personal experience. This trip was more recent. It happened after I came back from India in January 2023.

It was an atypical winter day in Surrey—no sun in sight and cold. I got a trip request in Surrey, and it led me down a strange back alley. As a driver, sometimes when I go to pick people up, I end up in strange places—sometimes it almost feels like I am driving right into someone's backyard. But if a passenger wants me there, I will go there.

This passenger had called me to the back of their house, as their place was on a busy street and only back-alley pickup was possible. When I arrived, she messaged me through the app that she was coming, but after over five minutes, she hadn't come to the car. Five minutes of staring at the door and expecting the passenger to step out any second—it gets bit frustrating.

Soon, an old African lady walked out with a big suitcase and apologized for making me wait. I grabbed her bag, and she went back to get her other bag. I placed all her luggage in the trunk, and we took off. She was going to the airport from Surrey—what else could I ask for? Those trips always paid well.

The passenger, who was in her late sixties, seemed to be impressed by my vehicle, as I was driving a new electric car. I asked her where she was going, and she explained that she was going to Philadelphia to see her son and grandson.

I asked her if she lived in Surrey by herself or if she had another child with her there. She told me she didn't live in Canada anymore; she had lived and worked in Canada for twenty years as a nurse, and now all four of her sons were settled in their lives. Her oldest son was forty-one years old and had two teenage kids. The youngest was around thirty-one and unmarried.

This made me wonder. "Why don't you live with one of your kids?"

"I used to," she told me, "but then I realized it was time to let go of things."

She explained, "As a parent, your kids always feel like your kids, regardless of how old they are. But you have to let them fly on their own without interrupting them. I was living with one of my married sons, and, knowingly and unknowingly, I ended up making myself part of their problems. I would want to know why they were fighting and, being a mother, sometimes you end up being a little biased toward your son.

"So, I moved out on my own. I'm retired and separated from my partner, and I didn't want to live in Canada anymore.

But you know, it can get lonely at times if you don't have your loved ones sticking their noses in your matters." She ended up buying a small house in Zimbabwe in her hometown. She said she was returning there after seeing her son. I asked her how she liked living back at home. She said she loved it at her little house; she had a small garden where she grew her own plants and vegetables. Though she was separated from her partner, she was still

Metered Moments

connected to her partner's family, and they still talked, attended weddings, and all stopped by her place sometimes.

"Yes," she said. "Zimbabwe might not offer the Canadian lifestyle, and it has some problems, but being at home gives me peace."

She said she came back once a year to get her health checked and meet her friends from nursing. Then, she meets her kids and goes back, letting them live their own lives but still being a part of them.

This is something I realized happens in Indian communities, and some of you might agree that it happens in yours as well. We hold onto the kids that we raised and we want to keep an eye on them. There is nothing wrong with that—it's love, after all. As for my parents, they still live with my brother in India, and I have heard them talk about fights between my brother and his wife. But the thing is, you don't need to be part of their fights, regardless of who's wrong or right. They are still figuring each other out—let them be.

Yes, if you are a parent, you have worked hard, and you have done enough for your children. Now, take it easy on yourself. Enjoy your life a little, especially if you are retired and if your health allows. Just enjoy this life, as my passenger was doing. That doesn't have to involve moving away from everyone—just whatever makes you happy. It could be simply taking a few trips a year, or staying in your community and doing things that you couldn't do while you were busy making money for your kids and giving them the best life, you could.

Do yourself a favor and take a trip. You will realize there are things you haven't done in decades. Let go of your worries and live a little.

Sincerity

This incident is close to my heart and always will be. I mean, at five years of driving an average of ten to twelve hours a day, five to six days a week, at least thirty trips per day? You can imagine the amount of people I have driven for, yet some passengers still manage to make a long-lasting impression.

In this special incident, I, for once, did not need to intervene much, as I realized I was in for a treat. I got a call from the Kerrisdale area, and when I arrived at the pickup location, an elderly couple entered my car. They settled down and I started driving.

Then came the classic question: "How are you guys and how's your day going?" Once the initial greetings were out of the way, I learned that they were heading to West Vancouver. I noticed the madame was not in a great mood—she gave out a vibe of "don't talk to me" and started looking out the window.

The sir, however, started chatting with me. "Are you married, son?" I told him no, not yet, and he said, "You know what is the most important thing to check before you marry someone?"

"What, sir?"

"Well, check her mental health. She needs to be mentally stable."

When he made this remark, the madame said, "You need to stop talking."

The sir said, whispering, "I think she forgot to take her medication. That's why she's going crazy."

"It's you who's crazy here, not me," she shot back. He jumped in again, saying that's what happened when she didn't take her medication.

After this, there was a little quiet moment where they both went silent, I guess in anger. They just looked in opposite directions. As I was enjoying this back and forth, I entered downtown Vancouver. Their brief pause ended as they realized the neighborhood we were in. The mood changed instantly from fighting to going down memory lane.

They fell into conversation about a restaurant they used to frequent and a store that had recently closed. They reminisced about a friend's old apartment and walks by the water they used to take together.

Love precedes everything, and, sadly, we tend to forget that. Let me tell you one thing very clearly: life is not those big moments that you look forward to. It's the little moments that happen while you are waiting for the big ones. Once again, that might be a cliché, but as usual, we should take its message seriously.

Love, forgive, laugh, repeat. We could all use some love. When we make mistakes, we hold onto them for years. We go hard on others and even harder on ourselves. In relationships especially, be kind to each other. Just because you have been with the same person for twenty years, you have no right to take it for granted. Treat each other with respect while maintaining mutual understanding. How could you treat the person you chose over the rest of the world to be your partner with cruelty? Love with all your heart, and forgive as soon as you can. Laugh together without any worries or judgement; laugh with all your heart. I feel that so-called "adults" often forget the fundamentals of life; we don't even express our emotions. Express them and do it sincerely.

Love, forgive, and laugh (sincerely).

What is Life without Friends?

You are in for a treat with this one. It's such a sweet little memory, and I'm glad for the chance to share it with you. I hope you take away the same joy and lesson from this story as I did.

It was a weekday morning around 5 o'clock. I was working and got a call from Kitsilano. It was always more likely someone looking to go to the airport in the early morning, and airport trips were pretty good money, so I was feeling hopeful.

My route led me to a "T" point at the end of the road, and, according to the map, I had to go right. Since it was still dark, it was hard to read house numbers, so I had to focus and drive slowly in order to find my passenger's address. As I scanned each house number, turning right at the "T," I was greeted by a black image.

I took a moment as I tried to understand what I was looking at. All I could seem to figure out was that it was a strange human figure dressed completely in black, and this figure was holding something.

I moved a little farther to see the figure from a better angle with some help from the streetlight. It was my passenger! She was elderly, and the thing she was holding onto was a walker so she could stand and wait for me. I got down to help her to get in the cab and buckle up, and I put the walker in the trunk. I started driving, and she told me that we needed to grab her friend.

She gave me pretty good directions to her friend's place, which surprised me, considering how dark it was. Spotting the house numbers was again an issue, but she brought us to the right place. Her friend came out within a minute. I helped this second passenger sit down and then took care of her walker as well.

As I started driving, they told me to drop them off at the nearby McDonald's. I drove along to their destination, and they started talking to each other. They spoke a language that I had never heard before, or at least I didn't hear them clearly enough to recognize it. I asked the first passenger what language they were speaking, and they informed me it was Greek.

From there, the conversation blossomed. Apparently, these two had been friends for a very long time, and that day, after having a McDonald's breakfast, they were grabbing the bus to go to Seattle, heading across the Canada-US border to shop. They both seemed like they could have been grand-mothers, but they got up early. The first passenger made sure to grab her friend, and then they enjoyed speaking in their own language. I'm sure they had a great day together.

Though I spent a short time with those women, they got me thinking about the importance of friendship. These are rela-tionships we think we choose, but perhaps it's actually fate,

Metered Moments

the mysterious ways of this universe, that brings us together. You have your friends' backs, and they have yours.

Friendships don't need to be tested. I consider myself lucky to have some great friends. They all play big roles in my life and I can't thank God enough for giving me such companions. Don't be shy—give yourself the gift of a friend. Be kind to yourself and be kind to others, and people who are like you will gravitate toward you. I hope you will all get this happiness. Friends are important. Very important.

Seoul-ful People

Thinking about this trip gives me butterflies in my stomach. A human interaction should always be this kind and gentle, something that brings out a smile each time you think about it.

Families, in my opinion, are often not easy to talk to, as they want to talk with each other. Even if I wanted to talk with them, it wouldn't be easy to drive and make eye contact for multiple conversations at once. Plus, when many people are taking a cab together, they often aren't going very far. Usually in this kind of situation, I just drive while eavesdropping on their conversation so I can hear what they are talking about. When the timing is right and I can unexpectedly add in something funny in their conversation, it's a treat for everyone.

This event happened in fall 2018. I picked up a family of four from downtown around 7 a.m. The son was running a bit late. The family consisted of parents and their two adult sons, and they were headed to the airport. I asked them what airline they were flying with, and they told me Korean Airlines. They were from South Korea and were visiting Vancouver for a few days, checking out the city and enjoying good food. They loved their time in the city and planned to come back again.

With the preliminary chat out of the way, I started focusing on driving, leaving dead silence in the car. Breaking the ice in a car full of adults sometimes feels like a hard job. I was still trying to think of what funny thing I might say to lighten the mood when the mother asked me where I was from. I told her I was from India, and she said I was very handsome—even her sons said I was good looking for a cab driver! I went blank for a second, but eventually managed, with red cheeks, to say thank you.

They also liked the fact that I could speak English very well. I told them I came from an area in India where we were given English by the British colonizers, and I was lucky enough to have studied in an English school and have parents who were graduates as well.

We were halfway through the journey when I asked them how the boys were doing. The mother told me one was working and the other one was still in school but eager to start work. I spoke with the boys too. We did chat a little about how they'd enjoyed this trip and they said they'd love to visit Vancouver during summer.

All in all, it was a simple, sweet conversation. Usually I'm grumpy so early in the morning—as, I like to say, it takes this car some time to warm up. But with just that little act of kindness and warmth, they made my day, and I remember them even after five years. Don't you ever underestimate those little acts of kindness—for you, they might be small things, but for someone else, they might change their entire day, and they might remember it for months or years! ***Maybe that little effort is not so little after all.***

Sky High

Some days, you're just in the zone; in some way or another, it's like you're directing what happens. This story takes place on one of those days. I was also excited for the evening, as I was going to see a concert with a friend.

I'd just finished dropping someone off at YVR, and as I drove off the airport ramp, I got a trip request from international pickup, so I went straight back there. The name offered me no clue as to who my passenger would be. When I arrived, there was a kid waiting with two big pieces of luggage. I helped him with his bags and we started the journey.

It was a trip to Surrey, so I couldn't have asked for a better end of the day. The passenger was a twenty-two-year-old from Sri Lanka in Canada for his studies. I don't even remember the first thing he asked me, but I remember the second: "Is weed legal here?" I laughed and said, "Yes, my boy, you made it. It's all legal here." I had another chuckle about this, but he was a good, sincere kid.

Fact: Your first contact, whoever comes to pick you up at the airport when you arrive in Canada for the first time, is someone you will remember forever. It's true! In my case, I still remember my sister-in-law and my brother outside with their two kids; their daughter was in my brother's arms and their son was next to his leg. I wanted to make sure this passenger remembered me as well.

I gave him a full verbal tour, from YVR to the mountains in Surrey. We discussed nature, Richmond, and Surrey, the speed limit on the highway, the Bollywood connection the Alex Fraser Bridge has, and Sri Lanka. He was so happy—this was heaven, and he'd made it. This was it.

We got to the address and I took the luggage, but the passenger went up to the wrong house. The passenger got worried, but I told him to try the place on our left, and it was the correct one. He came back with such a big smile, took his wallet out, and said, "How much?" I shook his hand and told him it was already paid for.

"Best of luck," I said. "Work hard, but enjoy your life." I watched him go inside and meet his new friend.

As I told this passenger about the best places to visit in Vancouver, how beautiful it is, and how the people are kind and friendly, I got to see it from a new perspective. It has always seemed pretty, but after you've seen it, the impact isn't as strong as the first time. We never look at it with the same wonder again, with all its shady evenings, the magic of the early mornings in rain, in cloudy weather, in scorching heat, or in fall, when nature is in the mood to paint.

Keep your eyes and your mind fresh. Look at the same places and people with a new view. Life will become full of color and excitement.

This passenger had the pure excitement and curiosity of a newborn. Keep that child alive and let it be curious. ***Let's not be so composed and collected. Get excited!***

Spiritual Seeker of North Vancouver

I wish you all were part of the conversation with this fine gentleman. He was traveling back to Calgary even though he'd just gotten back from London a few hours before. He was still wearing a mask, which I could understand, as he had been traveling frequently. He was a middle-aged chap, friendly as tea and biscuits. You must be wondering why I sound British all of a sudden; well, this passenger was yet another from England.

After a quick greeting, I started driving this man toward YVR. He seemed very energetic despite only getting a few hours' sleep. I started the conversation with the usual— how are you doing, and how's your day going? He simply told me he was tired, and then we talked a bit more about his life. He travelled a lot for work, and it usually kept him away from home and his three kids.

After touching on various other topics, spirituality came up. "I am not particularly religious," he told me, "but I am spiritual." I asked him what he had read on the topic so far, then mentioned some books and great speakers. "It's all about

69

energy and vibrations," he continued as we dove further into the topic.

I nodded. "I think so too."

I told him a story about a female passenger I'd picked up from downtown. She took some time to come down to the car from her place, and when she did, she had a big black bag, one used for long trips. As I drove her, she was fighting on the phone with someone—it sounded like a male friend, a typical one who wouldn't treat a woman with respect. I eventually dropped her off at her destination, but even after she left, I was feeling negative, like the aggression she had had seeped into me. My next passenger, though, was in a pleasant mood and smiled at me, and I felt good after she left.

Our British chap said that's exactly what he was talking about. I decided to get a little deeper, and asked him, "Do you know what the most precious thing in the world is? It's the eye, a naked eye, an eye so pure that it can see through all our judgements and our prejudices. To have such an eye is like a superpower that lets us see through the veils that we have created amongst ourselves."

He gladly agreed. I can't begin to explain the goosebumps I felt while getting to talk about these ideas. I felt great!

The chap smiled. This is increasing your vibration, brother. I think that we have to stay positive. ***What is happening is happening for our best.***

True Love

Life is what happens while you are working for your future. So, enjoy the journey—it's over, it's over. This trip reminded me of that, and it's a sweet memory that's still special to me. I hope that this kid is doing well and is safe.

It was a weekday morning, and the weather was chillier, as it was fall. The cooler fall weather is my favorite. It was still early—I started my shift around 4 a.m., as usual. I enjoyed the morning shift because there was less traffic and I could get off by 4 p.m. Airport trips are a favorite for any cab driver. They're quick trips, as passengers are in rush to get to the airport, and they are usually waiting for you right outside when you arrive. With the lighter traffic in the early morning, you can complete trips quickly, and, including tip, you could make thirty-five dollars in half an hour. The icing on the cake? Grabbing a steeped tea from Tim's on the chilly fall morning after making that thirty-five dollars in half an hour. Ahh—it can't get any better.

So, I was already happy to get a call for a trip to the airport from the Holiday Inn, not realizing this trip would get even better. I quickly made my way to the hotel so I didn't lose the passenger. When I got there, I saw a man holding a baby with a little bag beside him. I handled the luggage, and he settled in the car with the baby. I then started the journey to the airport.

I asked him how he was, how long he had been in the city, and if it was a work trip or leisure. I learned he had come with his wife and kid for a few days from a city on the east coast of the States, where his family had been living for about three years.

I don't remember the name of the city, but he told me that it was normal for him to hear gunshots every weekend downtown. For safety, he kept a gun in his locker at home. He said that he had never used a gun in his life, but he needed to keep one at home, just in case.

He then asked me about the situation in Vancouver. Was it safe to raise kids there? I was glad to tell him that Vancouver was almost perfect for raising kids. It was a safe place, and I had never heard gunshots. It wasn't as though there was no crime, but it wasn't bad enough that I needed to keep a gun in the house.

I told him the only flaw Vancouver had was its high cost of living. If cost was no issue, he should move to Van with his family. His kid was a couple of months old, still sleeping in his arms, and I felt the concern of this father who had lived in a dangerous place for three years. Now, as he looked at that same city from the perspective of raising kids, he had to reconsider his options.

This is what true love is: a father who wants to give his child a nurturing, playful, safe environment, even being willing to give up his home of three years to do so. In that spirit, I was just happy to give him a few details to help him make his decision.

I hope you moved to Vancouver and that now safety is no concern for you and your family. I hope you're living peacefully and complaining about how expensive it is, like the rest of us.

Perfect Ending

I am so glad we've made it this far. To be honest, I wouldn't have believed it if you told me when I was writing the first story that I would get this far. It is my honor to write this chapter. This story is living proof the universe works in mysterious ways to give us what we ask for. Let's start from the beginning. Trust me, you will enjoy it.

By this time, I was finished writing my target, which was twenty-two stories for my first book. A project very special to me as it was my first. Since editing was crucial, and with trust being a key factor, I turned to my cousin, a professional writer based in LA. I asked her if she would be willing to look over and edit my work. She agreed, and I sent her one of my stories to get started.

A week later she came back with the edited version of my story, and, holy—the things she fixed, and the many things she suggested for next time! I was very impressed by her work, so I asked her to edit my whole book. She responded after a few days, telling me that she was working full time as a copywriter and also volunteering as a writer for a few places, so even if she tried to edit my stories, she wouldn't be able to give them the time they deserved, knowing how important they were to me. She did, however, point me in the right direction by telling me about a website where you could hire people to edit for you. She also suggested I take a few writing courses to hone my skills.

First steps are usually hard to take. That's exactly how I was feeling—I checked the website, but I didn't know who to trust or who could deliver what I was looking for. After that step, I wasn't sure what to do next.

After writing this book I took a break and went to see, my family back in India. It was beautiful trip and gained some holiday weight as well. Coming back to Vancouver is always very hard as leaving loved ones behind.

It was my second day back to driving after coming back from India and I was at the end of my shift. Then I got—you guessed it—a trip from the YVR airport to Burnaby. That was perfect—after dropping her off, I could head home. I picked the passenger up, and we started our journey.

I asked her how her flight was, and she told me it was a disaster. You might remember when the US had the big mess with a flight system outage for a whole day across the country in January 2023—she was a victim of that. She made it to Canada, but she had to wait quite a bit. I asked her where she was coming from, and it turned out she was a grandmother on a trip to see all her grandkids from Regina to Denver to Burnaby. She herself was from Saskatchewan.

I asked her how life was in Saskatchewan, and she told me it was good. She lived in a town of seventy-five people, where everyone knew everyone, so it was good community living. She told me she was a special needs teacher all her life and had done her Ph.D. as well in this subject. I told her that, at one point, I was considering being a teacher, but for a guy starting

74

Metered Moments

from scratch in the most expensive city in Canada, a profession where it was unclear how long you'd be hopping around as a substitute teacher wasn't an option. Plus, to survive on a teacher's salary might be hard, especially in the beginning. She told me that if I were to become a special needs teacher, I could land a job quickly.

Rather than discussing the teaching job, I found myself talking about another passion of mine- my book. I poured my heart out, explaining how much it meant to me and my dream of seeing it published. As we reached her destination, I began unloading her bags. Stepping out of the car, she surprised me with "I would love to edit your book",

I couldn't believe it. She gave me her details and was excited to read my stories as she edited them. Over the next few weeks, I sent her two of my stories, and even though she was at her daughter's place to enjoy time with her grandkids, she still managed to edit my stories.

Soon, she had edited four of my stories. At that point, I thought she must have gone back to her hometown in Saskatchewan, and I decided to call her, as she was my editor, and I thought it would be nice to hear her voice and check up on her. When I called, she told me she was still in Burnaby. It was Wednesday evening when I called her, and she said she was going back to Saskatchewan on Friday afternoon and needed a ride from Burnaby to the train station in Vancouver. I said, "Don't you worry—I'll drop you off."

Friday at 12 p.m., I reached her daughter's place, and she was waiting for me outside. I packed her stuff in the car, and she decided to sit with me in front. We had a great chat.

Nipun Sharma

We reached the station, and I put her luggage on a trolley. I was about to push the trolley when she said to let her do it—she liked to do things on her own. I stood behind her as she went up to the counter checked her luggage. She told me to go back to work, as I needed to make money, but I told her it was OK—I wanted to see her off.

She had a confused look on her face, then she said I was very kind and helping her still. I wanted to tell her that this was how we did it back in India; if my elder relative was going somewhere, I would see them off, handle their luggage, and be with them until they boarded their train. Her train, however, wasn't for another hour, and she didn't like being looked after, so we parted ways. She wasn't sure when she would be in Vancouver again, but her eyes lit up when I offered to visit her in Saskatchewan. She said it was a great idea—I could bring my partner, and we could see the few festivals they have in the summer.

To this passenger: To be honest, in my Indian tradition, I would have touched your feet and given you a big hug, not because you helped me with this project, but simply because you were a kind person, and all I could ask for was your blessing. Just your hand on my head would do it. As usual, though, I was shy, and I didn't want to startle you by touching your feet.

We as humans are losing trust in one another. We often need a reason to trust each other, and if someone helps you out unprompted, you wonder, "Why are you doing this?" Before this era of technology, people were more open to each other. You could talk to a total stranger and have a

76

Metered Moments

conversation that you would remember for the rest of your life, one that might make you rethink how you saw the world so far.

My journey so far is testament to the fact that if we look past the prejudices that we carry and just simply talk to people, our road through this life will be smoother. Yes, we have to be safe, and we don't always know someone's intentions, but in a safe environment, if your heart allows you, I encourage you to talk. Open your heart and don't be fooled by appearance, age, sex, clothing, ethnicity, or skin color. Just talk, and you might just find a sense of warmth and connection in the most unexpected places and people. If I am still driving cabs while you are reading this book, and if I do end up picking you up, I would love to have a conversation with **YOU**.

Printed in the USA
CPSIA information can be obtained
at www.ICGtesting.com
LVHW010604220624
783721LV00010B/225